JANE HANSEN HOYT

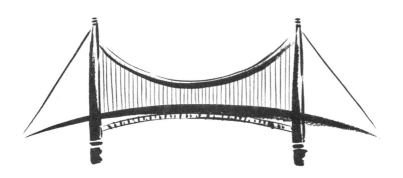

{ MASTER PLAN }

GOD'S ORIGINAL DESIGN
FOR MEN AND WOMEN

For information, contact:
Aglow International
www.aglow.org

Unless otherwise noted, all Scripture quotations are from the NEW KING JAMES VERSION. Copyright © 1979, 1980, 1982, Thomas Nelson, Inc.

Scripture quotations marked KJV are from the King James Version of the Bible.

Scripture quotations marked *The Message* are from *The Message: The New Testament in Contemporary English*. Copyright © 1993 by Eugene H. Peterson.

Scripture quotations marked NASB are from the NEW AMERICAN STANDARD BIBLE ®. Copyright © The Lockman Foundation 1960, 1962, 1963, 1968, 1971, 1972, 1973, 1975, 1977, 1995.

Scripture quotations marked AMP are from The Amplified Bible. Copyright © 1954, 1962, 1965, 1987 by The Lockman Foundation. Used by permission.

International Standard Book Number: 978-0-615-30079-5

Cover design by Vision Communications – Dallas, TX

Printed in the United States of America

1 2 3 4 5 6 7   15 14 13 12 11 10 09

Contents

Introduction

From Genesis to Revelation, it is clear that God is a God of eternal purpose. Job stated: "I know that You can do everything, and that *no purpose* of Yours can be withheld from You" (Job 42:2, emphasis mine).

In Isaiah 46:9, 10, God says: "Remember the former things of old, for I am God, and there is no other; I am God, and there is none like Me, declaring the end from the beginning, and from ancient times things that are not yet done, saying, 'My counsel shall stand and I will do all My pleasure.'" These words indicate to us that we can expect every prophetic purpose God has spoken since the beginning of time to be restored and fulfilled.

One such prophetic promise, spoken at the dawn of creation, will ultimately deal with the ancient curse against Satan in Genesis 3:15. While this verse refers directly to the woman, we understand that from the beginning God told us what dominion would look like in the earth. It was male and female. This was the structure God designed to deal with the enemy. This was the structure through which He would not only deal with Satan, but also reveal Himself to the world. It was "plan A," God's master plan. There was no "plan B."

The enemy, being aware of this plan, moved swiftly to separate the man and the woman, bringing distrust, fear, and suspicion between the genders to weaken, or attempt to render powerless, the plan of God.

The human race continues to suffer the fallout of Satan's malignant coup. The sad truth is, the Church itself has not fully recovered from this catastrophic event. The relationship between men and women, above all others, is the foundational place from which God will yet work to accomplish His ultimate intention. It is through the genders, male and female together, that God is fully revealed in glory, strength, power, and ultimate victory over the evil one.

The promise of Isaiah 60 is that, as the world grows darker, a brilliant light and glory will emerge simultaneously. It will be the light and glory of Almighty God arising in His people in a way that has not yet been seen.

This is one of those ancient promises that has yet to be fulfilled.

My great hope, as we look toward the days to come, is the certainty that God is building a strong and mighty, vibrant and victorious Church on earth—one that is destined to shine as a beacon of light through days of darkness and deception. One that displays the excellence of the King of kings and gives honor to the Lord of lords, and one He delights to call His glorious Bride.

A Current Reality

What an awesome time to be alive.

What an incredible time to be a son or a daughter of God.

What an excellent time to display the radiant testimony of the one true God!

We are living in a day of increased revelation. It is a time when God is bringing us into significant alignment with heaven. In his series, *The Way of the Warrior,* Graham Cooke calls this living "heaven to earth," not "earth to heaven." Ultimately, this is so the ancient promises and prophetic purposes of God can be fulfilled through us. We are the players in this final hour of time.

As I have often heard Graham Cooke say, "Prophecy is history written in advance. It unlocks the intentionality of

God." It declares to the world: "This is the way it will be"—and we get to be involved in the process.

The God of Restoration

God is forming something new in His people. Romans 14:17 states that, "the kingdom of God is . . . righteousness and peace and joy in the Holy Spirit." *The Message* states the same verse this way: God's Kingdom is about "what God does with your life as he sets it right, puts it together, and completes it with joy."

God is the God of restoration. His very nature is one of "setting things right." This is true not only in our personal lives, but it is also directly related to every purpose and promise He has ever stated in His Word, beginning in the Book of Genesis.

God established His plan and order for the human race from the beginning of time. It truly was "history written in advance" and it declares His intentionality. The very foundation of His plan was set forth in Genesis when the image of God was established as male and female. This was the structure through which God chose to reveal Himself and make Himself known in the earth.

> *God is the God of restoration. His very nature is one of "setting things right."*

The enemy has been hostile to this plan from the beginning. He has come against the foundation from the onset, and will continue his battle until he is finally thwarted and put under the feet of the genders, male and female.

Conflict, or war, is a strong and significant theme in the Bible and provides an important backdrop for God's entire story. We need to understand that the restoration of the

Church—male and female—will not take place in an atmosphere of peace, but will occur in the midst of conflict, due to the changing times around us.

Signs of the Times

As God's people, we see evidences of physical wars around us globally, and we sense the reality of the spiritual war that rages simultaneously. We speak of "the signs of the times" and wonder whether we are living in the last days. Even our news broadcasts and morning papers have been known to put an eschatological spin on reports of violence in the Middle East, asking whether we as a world are heading toward Armageddon.

As believers, you and I know that no one can accurately predict the end of the world. Nevertheless, throughout Church history, one of the constant questions on the hearts of God's people has been, "When will Jesus return?" and throughout world history, many have asked, "When will it all end?" Jesus Himself taught us in Matthew 24:36, 42: "But of that day and hour no one knows, not even the angels of heaven, but My Father only. . . . Watch therefore, for you do not know what hour your Lord is coming."

Though we cannot predict precisely "that day and hour," we are not left completely ignorant. Jesus instructed us to "watch," and we know from His teaching that when certain things happen, we can recognize that the close of the age is near: "And you will hear of wars and rumors of wars. . . . For nation will rise against nation, and kingdom against kingdom. And there will be famines, pestilences, and earthquakes in various places. All these are the beginning of sorrows" (Matthew 24:6–8).

The *New Spirit-Filled Life Bible* annotation for Matthew

24:8 teaches us that, "The term ['beginning of sorrows'] means 'labor pains,' which were expected to precede the end, making the transition from this age to the Age to Come. The severe labor pains, followed by delivery and fulfillment, are also a pledge of the end and of the joy at the time of 'delivery.'"

I believe we are feeling these labor pains, the "birth pangs" even now. It is a time of discomfort for many people in the Church; it is a time when many may be tempted to fear. As God's people, you and I are living in a different day—politically, economically, and socially. We are certainly living in an intense time, a more volatile time, than in days past. Even a decade ago, the world was a different place. We are living in a time of war on many fronts, and that has brought the Church into a new reality. Church is no longer "business as usual." Suddenly, it seems, everything has shifted. War, both natural and spiritual, has become a stunning reality. We are living in a time of conflict and great intensity, but it is an hour that is preparing us for the greatest victory and the greatest joy we have ever known.

Birth Pangs

Birth pangs are evident every time we turn on the news or pick up a newspaper. Think of the atmosphere in the world: nations are rising up against nations; the volatility of governments and economies is on the rise; terrorism and violence exist in ways we never dreamed possible years ago; new diseases pose serious threats to human life across the globe; cultures and ideologies are colliding with shocking intensity.

Think of the atmosphere in America: tense, anxious, "on the edge," and on alert. We live with the threat of terror—both from nations and ideologies outside our borders and within our borders, in the hallways and classrooms of our own schools. We live with the threat of violence in ways that never entered our minds ten, fifteen, or twenty years ago. In a very real sense, as I have mentioned, we are at war.

Conflicts rage throughout the Middle East, and from the border between India and Pakistan to the heart of Africa. Acts and fears of terrorism plague countries and cultures from the United States and Europe to tiny villages on small islands in Southeast Asia—and many places in between. We face cultural, social, political, and spiritual wars. They are the clash of two kingdoms.

Wars and rumors of wars are not the only indicators of the end of the age. Matthew 24:7 teaches us that the increase of natural disasters, "famines, pestilences, and earthquakes," is also a sign of the times. We see these destructive forces at work all

We face cultural, social, political, and spiritual wars. They are the clash of two kingdoms.

over the world with increasing intensity and frequency—famine in Africa, North Korea, and other countries; epidemics such as AIDS, SARS, and the diseases commonly called "bird flu" and "swine flu." In addition, we hear that earthquake activity has increased remarkably in recent years. In fact, one of the most dramatic earthquake events in recent memory occurred in 2004 and produced the tsunami that devastated Indonesia and affected more than seven other nations. This event destroyed families, wrecked economies, wiped out homes, and generally changed lives in radical ways that are almost impossible to comprehend.

In 2005, the United States suffered what weather authorities called the worst hurricane season on record. Hurricane Katrina tore through America's Gulf Coast leaving miles of devastation. Lawns where children once played became junkyards. The earthly treasures of men and women, boys and girls lay mangled, faded, torn, and often unrecognizable on soggy ground, leaving nothing more than the remnants of people's lives.

The birth pangs I have mentioned, and the intensity and frequency with which they are happening, indicate an escalation of events and speak of the prevailing conditions of this present age—all of which could well be precursors of the end times, indicating where we are on heaven's timeline. Intensity and frequency always indicate to a woman how close she is to the birth of her baby. Birth pangs also reveal that the process has begun, and will increase until the time the coming event has occurred. The same principle applies to us as we near the end of the age.

A Spiritual Shift

I believe everything we are seeing and experiencing in the natural world reflects a shift that has taken place in the spiritual realm. We do find ourselves in a different season than we have ever known. Many people in the Church are aware of it. Now the world is aware as well. Indeed, we have entered a different time globally, nationally, politically, economically, and spiritually.

Many of us want to respond to the crises of the world and the challenges of our lives as the prophet Habakkuk did:

O Lord, how long shall I cry, and You will not hear? Even cry out to You, "Violence!" And You will not save. Why do You show me iniquity, and cause me to see trouble? For plundering and violence are before me; there is strife, and contention arises. Therefore the law is powerless, and justice never goes forth. For the wicked surround the righteous; therefore perverse judgment proceeds. Habakkuk 1:2–4

Look anywhere in the world on any given day and you will see the birth pangs—wars and rumors of wars, pestilence, natural disasters, strife, and contention. Unrighteousness seems to be prevailing in many places, and indeed, the law seems powerless to bring the unrighteous to justice. But the Lord responds to the prophet, and would respond to us as well: "Look among the nations and watch—be utterly astounded! For I will work a work in your days which you would not believe, though it were told you" (Habakkuk 1:5).

As I stated in the Introduction, every purpose of God will be fully revealed and fulfilled. As we walk through this shift in the spiritual atmosphere, we are keenly aware that we are involved in the unfolding of these purposes. God is moving by His Spirit in a very strategic way to advance His Kingdom. It has always been His ultimate plan for dominion, power, and authority to be exhibited through men and women joined together in a victorious way against the enemy. Restoration has begun. What He set in place at the dawn of time is beginning to come forth.

> *Look anywhere in the world on any given day and you will see the birth pangs—wars and rumors of wars, pestilence, natural disasters, strife, and contention.*

Summary

- God is the God of restoration and He sets things right.
- God established the foundation of His plan and order for the human race from the beginning of time. It was set forth when the image of God was established as male and female, the structure through which God chose to make Himself known in the earth.
- The enemy has always been and continues to be hostile to God's plan.
- We are currently living in a time of natural and spiritual war on many fronts, and this reality has brought the Church into a new reality. This time of conflict and great intensity, the "birth pangs" we are experiencing, is preparing us to walk through the difficulties we face, knowing ultimate victory is ours.

Questions

1. Please go back to the section entitled, "The God of Restoration" and reread Romans 14:17 from *The Message*. How has God "set your life right"?
2. What was the foundation of God's original plan and order for the human race?
3. In what ways are you seeing the birth pangs described in this chapter in your own life and in the world around you?
4. How can you see God using the birth pangs currently taking place to bring restoration on earth?

Understanding God's Original Design

What exactly is God's original design for men and women? How did He create the male and the female to work together? He clearly revealed His plan and intention in Genesis 1:27, 28: "So God created man in His own image; in the image of God He created him; male and female He created them. Then God blessed them, and God said to them, 'Be fruitful and multiply; fill the earth and subdue it; have dominion over the fish of the sea, over the birds of the air, and over every living thing that moves on the earth.'"

From these verses, we can see that male and female were originally designed and created to express God's image on earth. They were to be fruitful, multiply, subdue the earth, and take dominion over it. Through them God intended to manifest Himself—His nature and His character, and His authority, displaying His indisputable power over the works of darkness, thus subduing His archenemy, Satan.

What Does This Mean?

The idea of "being fruitful and multiplying" is often applied strictly to the realm of marriage and family; while it does apply, it goes far beyond physical reproduction. To *multiply* means: "to be in authority, to enlarge, to increase." It is about the increase and multiplication of God's life and authority in us, individually and corporately—and it is about the will of heaven being brought forth on earth.

Note that God blessed the man and the woman. The meaning of the word *bless* extends far beyond our modern-day usage of it. The fact that God blessed them does not simply mean He wanted them to be happy and fulfilled and to enjoy their lives together. God was setting His structure in place, declaring His purpose, and revealing His heart intent toward mankind.

Let's take a closer look at this word. The word *blessing* means: "increase, fruitfulness, multiplication" and "prosperity." However, we must understand that it also means victory over our enemies. God spoke this word of blessing over the male and female. Through these two, Adam and Eve, God's intention was to establish His Kingdom on earth—to bring heaven to earth, to reveal Himself and to make Himself known in the earth. The word *blessing* is a very strong word, and as I have mentioned, it is an indicator of God's intent for them as a man and a woman. They were to walk in victory over their enemies, subduing and taking dominion over every foe that would arise against God's revealed plan. This is a thread that runs throughout the Word of God. It was set in place from the beginning.

We see the word *blessing* also spoken a little later over each of the patriarchs Abraham, Isaac, and Jacob, who represent the founding of the Nation of Israel. Therefore, we know that the word *blessing* is an important, strong word with great significance. Even as Adam and Eve were the "founding place" of God's creation, these men were a new beginning place of God, establishing for Himself a people on the earth to be His voice of authority, thus bringing heaven to earth. Because they were foundational to the establishing of "a people for God," this blessing typifies a spiritual principle that we, too, enter into as the descendants of Abraham. This principle of authority and dominion is woven throughout the Bible, beginning in the Book of Genesis through to Revelation.

Let's take a closer look at the words *subdue* and *dominion.* The word *subdue* means: to conquer, tread down, force, keep under, and bring into subjection. The word *dominion* means: to prevail against, to take or to rule over. Clearly, mankind was made to walk in authority. This was the word given to God's first "image bearers," the man and woman together. Satan had already fallen like lightning from heaven (see

> This principle of authority and dominion is woven throughout the Bible, beginning in the Book of Genesis through to Revelation.

Luke 10:18). This was the enemy they were being instructed to guard against, to subdue. Satan was the one who had boldly declared that he intended to "exalt [his] throne above the stars of God" and "be like the Most High" (Isaiah 14:13, 14). God had already declared war on His enemy. Satan's rebellion was to be dealt with. God would use mere humans to subdue the one who had formerly officiated in the heavenly realms.

Psalm 8:2, 6 underscores this fact: "Out of the mouth of babes and nursing infants You have ordained strength, because of Your enemies, that You may silence the enemy and the avenger. You have made him [humans] to have dominion over the works of Your hands; You have put all things under his feet."

Declaring War

From the time Lucifer rose up against God, declaring his intent to exalt himself above God, God's response was swift and very direct.

> "Your pomp is brought down to Sheol." . . . How you are fallen from heaven, O Lucifer, son of the morning! How you are cut down to the ground, you who weakened the nations! . . . "Yet you shall be brought down to Sheol, to the lowest depths of the Pit." Those who see you will gaze at you, and consider you, saying: "Is this the man who made the earth tremble, who shook kingdoms, who made the world as a wilderness and destroyed its cities, who did not open the house of his prisoners?"' . . . "The LORD of hosts has sworn, saying, 'Surely, as I have thought, so it shall come to pass, and as I have purposed, so it shall stand: that I will break the Assyrian [a type of anti-Christ spirit] in My land, and on My mountains tread him underfoot. This is the purpose that is purposed against the whole earth, and this is the hand that is stretched out over all the nations. For the LORD of hosts has purposed,

and who will annul it? His hand is stretched out, and who will turn it back?' Isaiah 14:11, 12, 15–17, 24–27

God had declared war on His enemy. Satan would be trodden underfoot. The eyes of God's people were to be opened to who he really is: the one who made the world a wilderness and brought destruction to its cities.

In Donald Barnhouse's book, *The Invisible War,* the events of Ezekiel 28:14–19 are described this way:

The great governing cherub had become the malignant enemy. Our God was neither surprised nor astonished, for, of course, He knew before it happened that it would happen, and He had His perfect plan ready to be put into effect. Although the Lord had the power to destroy Satan with a breath, He did not do so. It was as though an edict had been proclaimed in heaven: We shall give this rebellion a thorough trial. We shall permit it to run its full course. The universe shall see what a creature, though he be the highest creature ever to spring from God's word, can do apart from Him. We shall watch this experiment, and permit the universe of creatures to watch it, during this brief interlude called time. In it the spirit of independence shall be allowed to expand to the utmost. And the wreck and ruin which shall result will demonstrate to the universe, and forever, that there is no life, no joy, no peace apart from a complete dependence upon the Most High God, Possessor of Heaven and Earth.[1]

The earth has been made for humanity to rule over on God's behalf.

"It Is Not Good . . ."

Genesis 1:31 tells us that when God finished the work of creation, He "saw everything that He had made, and *indeed it was very good*" (emphasis mine). Obviously, He was pleased with the work of His hands. When the natural world was in place, we read that "the LORD God formed man of the dust of the ground, and breathed into his nostrils the breath of life; and man became a living being" (Genesis 2:7). God gave this man, Adam, the job of tending and keeping the Garden of Eden, with this instruction: "Of every tree of the garden you may freely eat; but of the tree of the knowledge of good and evil you shall not eat, for in the day that you eat of it, you shall surely die" (2:16, 17). In the next verse, God said, *"It is not good that the man should be alone;* I will make him an help meet [suitable] for him" (2:18, KJV, emphasis mine). Until this point, as God observed His creation, He pronounced it "very good." But now, something is "not good." What exactly was not good and why?

> *Adam's being* alone *seems to be the key thought in what God is expressing here as "not good."*

Adam's being *alone* seems to be the key thought in what God is expressing here as "not good." The Hebrew word translated *alone* literally means "separation." Man was not merely lonely; his "separation" was of a spiritual nature. To me, it speaks of an inner aloneness. George Berry's *The Interlinear Literal Translation of the Hebrew Old Testament* translates Genesis 2:18 this way: "Not good is being the man to his separation."[2] The question then becomes, separated from what or whom? At this point, the only other beings present with him were the animals. Could it be that this statement by God was not a mere observation of Adam's "loneliness," as some have assumed? Rather, far more seriously, it was addressing Adam's relationship with God Himself.

Adam had not yet been joined to God in His "divine life." For Adam to fulfill the purpose of God, to walk in authority over the enemy, He had to become a partaker of divine life. He was, at this point, merely a created being. God could not thrust divine life upon Adam; Adam would have to choose to receive it. But the future of God's plan depended on it.

Watchman Nee states in his book, *Messenger of the Cross:*

Of all the edible trees, this one (the tree of life) is the most important. This is what Adam should have eaten first. Why is this so? The tree of life signifies the life of God, the uncreated life of God. Adam is a created being, and therefore he does not possess such uncreated life. Though at this point he is still without sin, he nevertheless is only natural since he has not received the holy life of God. The purpose of God is for Adam to choose the fruit of the tree of life with his own volition so that he might be related to God in divine life. And thus Adam would move from simply being created by God to his being born of Him as well.[3]

When God said that Adam's aloneness was "not good," He meant it really was *not good*. There was a problem in paradise and God purposed to resolve it. Help was on the way.

Summary

- Male and female were originally designed and created to express God's image on earth. Because God blessed them, they were to be fruitful, multiply, subdue the earth, and take dominion over it.
- Mankind was created to walk in authority.
- Satan was the enemy the male and female together were to guard against and subdue.
- God uses mere humans to subdue the one (Satan) who had officiated in the heavenly realm.
- Adam's aloneness was not good.

Questions

1. According to Genesis 1:27, 28, what were God's instructions to the male and female? How do we see them being fulfilled today?
2. Who does God want to use to overcome the enemy? Why can we be confident that we can overcome him?
3. How have you experienced victory in the midst of difficulties in your life?
4. Why was Adam's aloneness not good?

A Suitable Helper

When God said, "It is not good that the man should be alone; I will make him an help meet for him" (Genesis 2:18, KJV), He was observing a need and His response was to make a help suitable for him. So He took from his side a bride, the foreshadowing of another bride that was yet to come. The Church, the Bride of Christ was taken from the side of Jesus. He gave us life. We are His Body, an extension of Himself in the earth (see Ephesians 5:30).

So, God created Eve—a woman like Adam in terms of her humanity, but radically different from him in other ways. She wasn't more than or less than Adam. She was simply different. God had fashioned her and made her what she needed to be to walk with Adam as his other self—his counterpart. They were, in today's language, "made for each other." She was God's idea and together they were God's design for the fulfillment of His plan of subduing the earth and taking dominion over it. God called her a help that was "meet," meaning "suitable" and adequate for him, one who could come alongside him and walk with him in a deeply purposeful way.

Divine Help, Human Help

The Hebrew word for help, *ezer*, means: "to surround, to protect, to aid, succor." Webster's definition of *succor* is "help, to run under, to give aid or assistance in time of distress." *Help* or *ezer* is an extremely strong word, used twenty-one times in Scripture. Sixteen times it refers to divine help (God Himself) and five times to human help, but always in the context of help in time of trouble or help against one's enemies. The use of the word itself reveals God's intent in sending Adam a help. God had fashioned the woman in such a unique way that she would be used to surround and protect Adam. There was a mighty call on his life—and now on their lives together. God had commissioned them to rise and walk in victory over the enemy.

Isn't it interesting that God didn't send Adam a fishing buddy, a basketball team, a boss, a brother, a father, or a coach? He sent him a woman because then, as now, it is the woman who is uniquely crafted by God to touch his heart, to engage his heart, and to help him open his heart to her and to God.

When God brought forth Eve in the earth, Adam immediately recognized her as "bone of my bones and flesh of my flesh" (Genesis 2:23). He recognized something of himself in her. She brought to Adam something that he needed. She was, of course, both human and divine help, but the emphasis was on the divine quality of the help she brought to Adam. The *Theological Wordbook of the Old Testament* says, "While this word designates 'assistance' it is more frequently used to designate 'the assistant' (as with Eve). As to the source of help, this word generally is used to designate 'divine help or aid.'"[1] In Psalm 121:1 the word *help* reflects this definition: "I will lift up my eyes to the hills—from whence comes my help? My help comes from the LORD, Who made heaven and earth."

Eve represents both human and divine help in that she was fashioned and sent from the hand of God. She is not the man's savior, but she can be used to open and engage his heart in relationship at a deeper level, hence, bringing him out of his aloneness. God was giving the man help for himself, for his own person. God makes it plain when He says, "I will make him an help

> *She was fashioned by the Father's hand and sent from His heart into a situation that needed help, a specific need He saw in Adam's life.*

meet [or suitable help] *for* him" (Genesis 2:18, KJV, emphasis mine). She will also complete him in their role as dominion takers—those who move in divine displacement of God's enemy, Satan. She was fashioned by the Father's hand and sent from His heart into a situation that needed help, a specific need He saw in Adam's life—to "surround, protect, aid, succor" the man, thereby bringing him into a relationship with her and, ultimately, fellowship with God.

Side by Side

When God looked upon the need created by the fact that Adam's aloneness was not good, and intentionally committed to make him a help "suitable" for him, He "caused a deep sleep to fall on Adam, and he slept; and He took one of his ribs, and closed up the flesh in its place. Then the rib which the Lord God had taken from man He made into a woman, and He brought her to the man" (Genesis 2:21, 22).

When we think of Adam and Eve, especially of her role in his life, we must remember that she was not fashioned from a place under Adam's foot. She was not taken from his shoulder, his elbow, his hip, or some other part of his body, but she was drawn from a significant portion of his body—his side—because she was created to walk side by side with him. She was crafted to come forth and walk side by side with him in a meaningful, powerful, authoritative way, so the two of them together would be fruitful, be blessed, and walk in dominion in the earth.

Eve's creation from the side of Adam teaches us that she was part of him, an extension of himself. When she was created, part of him was removed and returned to him in a very different package. The woman was not formed of new elements; she was not taken from the dust, hence, separate or independent from the man in that sense. She was part of who he was. He understood this, and delighted in it, saying: "This is now bone of my bones and flesh of my flesh; she shall be called Woman, because she was taken out of Man" (Genesis 2:23).

> *Eve's creation from the side of Adam teaches us that she was part of him, an extension of himself.*

It is interesting to note that the name given to the woman—*Eve*—is taken from a Hebrew word that also denotes verbal communication. Her name *Chavvah* means "life-giver," but the verb form is *chavah*, which is consistently translated as "declare" or "shew" verbally. She was uniquely and specifically designed to stand before him in an intimate, face-to-face relationship. She was designed to talk to him, to encourage and challenge him in love, using life-giving words. God intended her to surround and protect something of His creation that was very precious in His sight, the heart of man—his thoughts, his feelings, his inner self.

The virtuous woman described in Proverbs 31 is often referred to on Mother's Day in a sweet, sentimental way. Yet the strength and value of the woman spoken of in this passage is perhaps not fully realized: "An excellent [virtuous] wife, who can find? For her worth is far above jewels. The heart of her husband trusts in her, and he will have no lack of gain. She does him good and not evil all the days of her life" (Proverbs 31:10–12, NASB).

The Hebrew meaning of the word *virtuous (chaylil)* is: "force, strength, able, power, might," and describes her as coming with the strength of an army. Think of it. One woman, coming with the strength of an army! She was made for war. She was able, with her force, strength, might, and power, to come against any enemy that would arise against her family. Remember, God told us what dominion would look like in the earth; and it was male and female. Here, we are describing the powerful strength of "his other self, his other half." God had called them together.

This unique creation of woman from the side of the man was the beginning point of God's family, the emerging of the foundation of the House of the Lord and what would ultimately become the Church. As we read their story, we see unfold before our eyes a microcosm of the structure God chose to use on earth to display His glory and make His presence known. The foundation was male and female, the two were incomplete without each other—the two would together express the image of God. Out of this inaugural union, His glorious purposes would unfold and be manifest.

God's Image Expressed

When God created Adam, He made him in the full image of Himself. But when God took the woman from the side of the man, what happened to that image of God? Was it added to? Was it subtracted from? It was neither. It was divided. And now, for the image of God to be seen and felt and known and heard and observed in the earth, it must come through both the man and the woman. As they stood together in the garden, this was a picture of the Church to come. Male and female together comprised the structure through which God chose to begin to reveal Himself and make Himself known in the earth. It could never come through men alone; it could never come through women alone. It has to be expressed through the two of them together.

... for the image of God to be seen and felt and known and heard and observed in the earth, it must come through both the man and the woman.

From the beginning of the world, God has shown us what dominion would look like. It is male and female. "Together you will take dominion in the earth," He says. We cannot have true dominion, nor can we see the full image of God without both men and women. We cannot have one without the other. Again, I am not simply referring to the marriage union. I am referring to the relationship between the male gender and the female gender. *Together* we make up the Church. *Together* we will take dominion in the earth.

In the beginning, God expressed His purpose for male and female through a man and wife, but we must realize that His plan extends and should function both within the marriage union and beyond it to every area of life and relationships. The first man and the first woman were called together to be fruitful and to take dominion on earth. Today, men and women are still called together. We are still called to be blessed and to be fruitful. For some this happens primarily through a marriage relationship. For some, it happens in non-romantic partnerships in which men and women work together as a team to accomplish God's purposes. No matter how men and women work together, the kind of unity modeled in the garden results in great authority, great anointing, and great advancement of God's Kingdom on earth.

Summary

- Eve was God's answer to Adam's aloneness. She was not "more than" Adam or "less than" Adam. She was simply different.
- Adam and Eve together were God's original dominion takers. The relationship between the two of them was the structure through which His enemy, Satan, would be defeated.
- Eve represents both human and divine help to Adam. She was created as a suitable helper for him, to walk side by side with him in a powerful and purposeful way.

- Adam and Eve together express God's image. The fullness of His image cannot be seen in the male alone or in the female alone.
- True dominion over the enemy must be expressed through male and female together.

Questions

1. Recognizing that both men and women are created by God for specific purposes, how do you describe the differences between men and women?

2. How is the image of God manifested differently through men and women?

3. I have stated that God wants to use men and women together to fulfill His plan both within and beyond the marriage relationship. How can you envision this working outside of marriage?

The Strike

At the dawn of the human race, the foundation of God's plan was set in place. Together Adam and Eve bore the image of God. Together they were to be an expression of dominion and heaven's authority in the earth. Together, yet in uniquely different ways, each gender would express God's heart. This was the structure God chose. Without their comprehending this glorious plan, without their walking in the strength of this design, God's plan would fail. He has no plan B; there is only plan A, and it is God's master plan. That plan has not changed. God still desires that the Church truly comprehend the strength and power of His original design, that of the genders truly walking as one.

An Attempt to Undermine God's Plan

I do not think it was happenstance that the enemy approached the woman first in the garden. He who led the rebellion in heaven now seeks to continue it on earth. He was after the plan of God. He wanted to exalt himself above the Most High God.

Satan was present when the words of God were spoken forth in the garden. He heard God say that man's aloneness was not good. He knew that God had fashioned a "help" suitable for man—a help who would walk with him and, most importantly, be the expression of dominion in the earth with him that God had intended. He knew that she had a highly significant place in man's life and in God's plan, and he knew that God's intention for them was to be blessed, to be fruitful, to multiply and to conquer, tread down, keep under, prevail against, bring into subjection, and rule over any opposing force that would arise in the earth to counter the plan of God. This is what it means to take dominion.

In approaching the woman first in the garden, perhaps Satan knew that in order to disrupt the plan of God, his best strategy would be to *attack the help God sent*. Satan ultimately purposed to silence the woman, to render her useless and powerless in the man's life, but further, to so weaken her in God's ultimate plan that the whole plan of God would be ineffectual.

> *In approaching the woman first in the garden, perhaps Satan knew that in order to disrupt the plan of God, his best strategy would be to attack the help God sent.*

One only has to look at the breakdown of the family structure and society, the growing rejection of long-accepted morals and standards, and the war against the definition of marriage as a union between a man and a woman to realize that we are in a spiritual war beyond anything the Church could have imagined in past times. Why are biblical truths and Christian values being attacked as they currently are? This is not just a political war, but a spiritual war of great proportions. The liberal press, the gay agenda, and the rise of Islam in the world are not just threats to Christianity, but also strikes against God Himself. They represent an anti-Christ spirit that is coming against the very plan of God, the very structure He set in place from the beginning—that of the union, the strength, the dominion God intended for the man and woman. The Church must see what is taking place and begin to move into a greater place of authority, but that cannot happen without the Church's first seeing the strength of the place of the woman and the help she was designed to be not only in a marriage union, but also as a voice within the Church, the family, and society. Neither can her influence nor her voice be minimized. It is the hour for the Church to awaken and arise to its fullest capacity and take dominion.

Satan's Suggestion

Satan makes his appearance in the Garden of Eden in the form of a serpent and introduces to Eve the mere suggestion that perhaps God is withholding something from her (see Genesis 3:1–6). He does not appear in the guise of a scary-looking monster or an intimidating giant. He does not scream or shout. He shows up as a snake—not an unusual sight in a garden—and wins Eve's trust not with a blaring accusation, but with a simple suggestion.

I can imagine it might have happened something like this. Eve is walking along through the garden. It is lush; it is beautiful; it is peaceful; it is paradise. She is innocent and pure, untouched and uncorrupted by sin. But she had been warned. She knew God had said not to eat of the fruit of the tree in the midst of the garden, also known as the "tree of the knowledge of good and evil." She and Adam were free to eat the fruit of any tree in the entire garden—except that one.

She knew it; and Satan knew she knew it.

In his charming, clever way, he slithered up to her and asked: "Has God indeed said, 'You shall not eat of every tree of the garden'?" (Genesis 3:1).

Eve immediately responded: "We may eat the fruit of the trees of the garden; but of the fruit of the tree which is in the midst of the garden [the tree of knowledge of good and evil], God has said, 'You shall not eat it, nor shall you touch it, lest you die'" (Genesis 3:2, 3).

With crafty dialogue and one strategic question, Satan planted in Eve's mind the idea that God might be withholding something good from her and Adam. Eve began to ponder his suggestion, taking closer notice of the tree, probably thinking along these lines: *Perhaps God is withholding something. Maybe He just doesn't want to share what's on that tree. Perhaps there is something more that I need to help me fulfill my purpose. Maybe I could get it with just a bite or two of fruit from that forbidden tree.*

> With crafty dialogue and one strategic question, Satan planted in Eve's mind the idea that God might be withholding something good from her and Adam.

Ever the sly one, the serpent gently pressed on, blatantly lying to Eve and defying God: "You will not surely die. For God knows that in the day you eat of it your eyes will be opened, and you will be like God, knowing good and evil" (Genesis 3:4, 5).

Because she turned from God and allowed Satan to influence her, Eve then "saw that the tree was good for food, that it was pleasant to the eyes, and a tree desirable to make one wise" (Genesis 3:6a). And the next thing we know, Eve, acting in her own wisdom, on her own accord, outside of the expressed word and will of God, "took of its fruit and ate. She also gave to her husband [who was] with her, and he ate" (Genesis 3:6b).

The Aftermath

Satan had staged a coup; it was a masterstroke, a bull's-eye! Satan had accomplished his purpose. *He had conclusively separated them from the one source of life that was stronger than he.* Adam and Eve had been commanded to "freely partake" of the Tree of Life, which was the life of God. For Adam to become a partaker of divine life he must freely partake as he had been commanded (see Genesis 2:16). "Freely" did not imply "free to do it or not." Adam was to eat a lot, freely and plentifully of the trees God had provided for his sustenance and strength, most specifically, of the Tree of Life. Adam, having free will, could choose not to eat of the provision God had made, but it would be in direct disobedience to the command.

God the Father was urging Adam to partake of His life, the provision for Adam to be able to stand against his enemies. God knew what disastrous results he would suffer if he refused to partake. Brokenness. Pain. Loss of peace. Death, even while living. God wanted to establish him in his sonship—not just a created son with the breath of God in his being, a living soul, but a living spirit with the life of God flowing within him, empowering, enabling, and enriching every facet of his life. Satan turned them to their own wisdom, their own way, the way of the flesh, in which "nothing good dwells" (Romans 7:18). He successfully turned their focus away from God and onto themselves as the center of their lives. The fruit of their action was instantaneous: broken relationship. Satan turned the intended combined strength of the genders—which is what God intended—into confusion, fear, and mistrust.

In the wake of their sin, they realized they were naked and they experienced shame. They scurried to cover themselves, to hide from the presence of God. Can you imagine the disbelief and horror that must have registered in their hearts and minds as they gained the ability to recognize good and evil? Having partaken of the fruit that gave them such knowledge, having eaten it and chosen it as their life source, they now had an intimate knowledge of both good and evil deep within their beings. Their lives would never be the same.

> *He successfully turned their focus away from God and onto themselves as the center of their lives. The fruit of their action was instantaneous: broken relationship.*

It is important to note that God never intended Adam and Eve to remain ignorant of good and evil. He always wanted them to know the difference. Isaiah 7:15 tells us that when Jesus—our perfect example—came, He would know how to "refuse the evil and choose the good" from an early age. God always intended for Adam and Eve to choose His Spirit (represented by the Tree of Life) as their source of life and wisdom, rather than putting upon themselves the pressure of discerning between good and evil and looking to their inadequate humanity as their source of life.

After they ate from the tree of the knowledge of good and evil, they lived from their "self-centers." What they judged to be good or evil would be determined by the immediate effect it had on them. Whatever felt good, looked good, tasted good, or seemed good to them would be deemed "good." Whatever felt bad, looked bad, smelled bad, or gave them a bad experience would be deemed "bad." They—without the benefit of divine wisdom, eternal perspective, or God's insight—would choose what was good and what was bad.

This incident in the garden, which we know as "the Fall," proves the point: "You Gotta Serve Somebody." Although Bob Dylan, who penned those words, is no prophet, this song title of his is true. By choosing to go their own way, Adam and Eve effectively placed themselves not under their own authority, but under the rule of Satan. They changed kings—from God to Satan; they changed kingdoms—from the Kingdom of light to the kingdom of darkness; and they ensured that all their descendants, including you and me, would be born into a fallen condition, under the rule of our enemy.

Summary

- When Satan wanted to undermine God's plan, he first approached the woman, knowing that she was not only essential to His plan, but also necessary to the man.
- Satan's goal in the garden was to separate Adam and Eve from their life source, God Himself. He

accomplished this with the simple suggestion that God was withholding something from them.

- Separated from God, Adam and Eve had to rely on their own wisdom and knowledge, without the benefit and power of God's insight and perspective. This placed Adam and Eve out from under the loving rule of God and under the rule of Satan instead.

- Adam and Eve's separation from God ensured that all who would be born after them would be born into a fallen condition, separated from God.

Questions

1. The enemy first approached the woman in the garden partly because she was so important to the man. Why and how is the woman necessary to the man?

2. What was the most tragic result of the fact that Adam and Eve believed Satan's suggestion?

3. Have you ever relied on your own wisdom instead of God's? What were the results?

The Ancient Curse

As the leader of one of the largest and most influential women's ministries in the world, I grieve as I travel the globe and see the hardships women endure. My heart breaks for those who are ignored, overlooked, oppressed, and abused, and for those who suffer under the tyranny of intimidation, control, and disregard as a way of life. I cringe when I hear about cultural customs that mutilate a young girl's sexual organs, leaving her in pain for the remainder of her life. I am outraged when I see women who must wear coverings from head to toe with only enough of an opening so they can see—all for the purpose of keeping men from lusting. I am deeply saddened and troubled when I read the statistics, and hear about the realities of many women I know personally who, as little girls, were sexually used and abused by fathers, uncles, brothers—those who were supposed to protect them—and see that such abuse leaves pain and shame that can affect them for the rest of their lives. I am shocked and angered when I hear the horror of "honor killings," the taking of a woman's life to "preserve" in some twisted way the "honor" of the men in her family.

Have you ever wondered why there is such violence and wrath poured out against women in so many cultures of the world? Through the ages, the enemy has come against women for a very specific reason. I believe he has feared us since the very beginning of human history.

We can see this in nations and societies across the globe; we can see it within the Church; we can see it even in America, which seems to be so liberated and advanced. In many places, an attitude of oppression exists that is difficult to define, but undeniably real. When it's present, women feel it; they know it; they sense it every time they encounter forces at work to suppress their influence and silence their voices.

The Siege

The abuse of women lays siege to the entire human race. The abused and violated suffer unspeakably at the hand of the enemy, and I want you to understand what he is doing in our day. He did not discontinue his operations against women when he finished with Eve; he has never let up in his efforts to silence and harm women.

The abuse of women lays siege to the entire human race.

As of 2007, approximately one-third of the 3.3 billion females on earth were being abused or would be abused at some time in their lives. That's one out of every three women. Just think about the last time you attended a friend's birthday party. Imagine sitting at lunch or in a coffee shop with your two closest female friends. While it may not be true for the three of you, statistically speaking, one of you would be an abused woman. Staggering, isn't it?

Even more staggering is that, according to such groups as the United Nations, Amnesty International, and Human Rights Watch, the abuse I refer to includes sexual assault, mutilation, beating, false imprisonment, and slavery—and those statistics apply not only to women in the prime of life, but also to infants, children, teens, and elderly women. Serious stuff.

I, for one, do not agree with the world's rationale for abuse. I believe the reason so many women are abused predates the religious systems and cultural practices of our day. It started in the garden!

Exposed!

Genesis 3 reveals the reason for the ongoing abuse and suppression of women throughout history and to this day. This is when the enemy became so enraged at Eve. This is where the "ancient curse" is first revealed, and it explains the violent treatment of women and the hatred and abuse of women that encircle the globe and are present in every culture in the world.

Remember, we have said that the enemy approached the woman first in the garden, with the intent of attacking the plan of God. His thrust was primarily against God, but he went at God through his subtle approach toward the woman, the help God had sent.

Following the tragic events of that day, God came in

the cool of the evening, calling out to them saying, "Where are you?" Adam responded first. He began to squirm and hedge, blaming it on Eve, saying, "The woman whom You gave to be with me, she gave me of the tree, and I ate" (Genesis 3:12). Then God directs His words toward Eve, asking, "What is this you have done?" Eve responds decidedly, "The serpent *deceived* me, and I ate" (Genesis 3:13, emphasis mine). God immediately responded to Eve's admission with thunderous, explosive, and enduring words of division between Satan and the woman. He began where the sin began, with the serpent: "You are cursed more than all cattle, and more than every beast of the field; on your belly you shall go, and you shall eat dust all the days of your life" (Genesis 3:14).

Notice that it was the woman who first exposed the enemy for who he really is. She said, "He *deceived* me and I ate." She nailed him. She called him who he really is—the deceiver. She had exposed God's enemy. And God spoke into that, and in essence He said, "Now forever and ever, Satan, down through the ages and down through the centuries she will be used again and again and again to expose you, to uncover you, and to call you who you really are!" He said, "She will be your enemy. You can count on the fact that forever and ever she is going to recognize you in family situations; she is going to recognize you in the Church; and she is going to recognize you in the world. She is going to know where you are working and what you are up to."

> *Notice that it was the woman who first exposed the enemy for who he really is.*

Who's Whose Enemy?

Satan heard it and he understood! The woman would be his enemy. While he would continue to deceive her into thinking *he* was *her* enemy, the exact opposite would be the truth: she was his enemy.

Genesis 3:15 states it this way: *"I will put enmity between you and the woman,* and between your seed and her Seed; He shall bruise your head, and you shall bruise His heel" (emphasis mine). The *American Heritage Dictionary* defines *enmity* as "deep seated, often mutual hatred." God was saying, in no uncertain terms: "I will put deep, mutual hatred between you, Satan, and the woman; between your seed and her Seed, and there will come a Seed from the woman that will utterly destroy you. It will be a death blow to your head. You can count on it. And you can look for it to come through the woman. The seed that comes from you will merely bruise the heel, but what comes from her will thoroughly demolish you."

This is the reason for the hatred and violence against women. It comes from the pit of hell. It is Satan's ongoing attempt to silence the female gender and to render us powerless.

The woman would remind him again and again to "stay on his belly and eat dust!" The enmity God put between the woman and Satan began in the garden and continues to this day. The deal was done: she would crush his head and continue to expose him throughout the ages. This has led to systematic attempts—both flagrant and subtle—to silence, suppress, and undermine the woman's value as a person and her role in families and societies around the world. This is the reason women are not only abused, but overlooked, often kept uneducated, not taken seriously, denied opportunities, and forbidden to follow their dreams. Sadly, the Church often does not recognize the strength of the woman's role, and she is kept serving in the nursery or singing in the choir. Even as women in the Middle East are kept under burkas, women in the Christian community are often bound by a "religious" burka, a religious system that can be limiting spiritually to the "other half" of the Body of Christ.

Just as I do not believe the world rightly understands the reasons behind the oppression and hatred of women, I also do not believe the world provides the best solutions to it. We must avail ourselves of the resources we have to assist abused women, but we must also move beyond the help the world offers. What do we do? We help women understand their authority over the evil one. We teach them that they can overcome him. This, in my mind, is the key to their destinies and the best solution to the strike he has carried out against women for centuries.

Summary

- For generations, the enemy has feared and come against women for a very specific reason. This is evident around the world and has been throughout human history.
- The abuse of women deeply and radically affects the entire human race.
- Eve, the woman, first exposed Satan for who he really is. Women continue to expose him to this day, and he continues to fight back against them.
- Women must understand and exercise their authority over the enemy. This is a key to their destinies.

Questions

1. How does the abuse of women lay siege to the entire human race?

2. According to Genesis 3, what is the reason for the abuse and hatred of women that exists in the world today?

3. What is the ancient curse and how does it continue to operate today?

4. What are some ways God uses women to expose the enemy today—in families, in communities, in churches, in the marketplace, in leadership roles, and in society in general?

5. Can you see how being able to overcome the enemy is a key to your destiny? In what ways is this true for you?

Divine Displacement, God's Way

God conceived an eternal plan before the foundation of the world. Mankind, male and female, was made for authority. We were created and fashioned for dominion. We were given rulership of the earth. Through Adam's choice to live by the wrong tree, the tree of the knowledge of good and evil, rather than the Tree of Life, Satan staged a coup and man gave Satan a legal place in the earth and in his life. Through his rebellion, God's enemy, Satan, brought all things into chaos. God quickly and decisively declared how this rebellion would be dealt with. Through the woman, the very one he had initially deceived, a Seed would come that would bring a death blow to his head, utterly destroying him. By the masterstroke of God, He would redeem and reconcile things back to His original purpose, thereby restoring mankind to His original purpose—again giving them the opportunity to choose to eat from the Tree of Life, through His Son Jesus Christ.

Power and Authority

In his book, *Authority in Prayer,* Dutch Sheets speaks about the issue of God's governmental authority: "The question of who's in control is a governmental issue. We often think of government only in its civil sense, but Webster's defines *govern* as 'to direct and control; to regulate by authority; to influence; to direct; to restrain; to steer or regulate the course of; to exercise authority; to maintain the superiority.'"[1]

Sheets defines *power* as the "strength or force needed to rule" and *authority* as "the 'right' to do so."[2] He goes on to say: "Satan didn't gain any power at the fall and didn't lose any at the cross. His power or ability didn't change at either event; his authority, or the right to use that power, *did.* . . . Scripture nowhere says that Christ delivered us from or dealt with Satan's power at Calvary. *He dealt with Satan's authority.*"[3] When Jesus rose victorious from the grave He had faced the opposition of "the powers of the air." That means all principalities; every power, might, and dominion; every name that is named not only in this age, but also in the age that is to come. Every opposing force that stood against God's purpose had been overthrown!

Yes, Eve was the first to be ensnared by Satan and the first to expose his true nature. She was also the subject of the first promise of deliverance. When things looked hopeless to the human mind, God had a way. "When the fullness of the time was come, God sent forth his Son, made of a woman, make under the law, to redeem them that were under the law, that we might receive the adoption as sons" (Galatians 4:4, KJV). Through the Seed of the woman, "[sin and] death [would be] swallowed up in victory" (1 Corinthians 15:54). Through the Seed of the woman, God would "[disarm] principalities and powers, [making] a public spectacle of them, triumphing over them in it" (Colossians 2:15). Heaven and earth's greatest victory would be realized out of the greatest point of defeat.

Yes, Eve was the first to be ensnared by Satan and the first to expose his true nature. She was also the subject of the first promise of deliverance.

When Jesus, the perfect Seed, came forth through woman, and then the Seed went down into death, it looked as though Satan had won again. Acts 2:24, however, says, "[But] God raised Him up, liberating Him from the pangs of death, seeing that it was not possible for Him to continue to be controlled or retained by it" (AMP). It was not possible for the grave to hold Him. "I am He who lives, and was dead, and behold, I am alive forevermore. . . . And I have the keys of Hades [hell] and of Death," Jesus declared to John in Revelation 1:18. Jesus had come forth from death victoriously, bringing with Him the legal right for humanity to again exercise on earth the delegated dominion God had given them.

Jesus spoke powerful words to His seventy amazed followers who had been sent out two by two. After going from city to city, they said to Him, "Lord, even the demons are subject to us in Your name." Jesus' response was, "I saw Satan fall like lightning from heaven! Behold, I give you the authority to trample on serpents and scorpions, and over all the power of the enemy, and nothing shall by any means hurt you" (Luke 10:17–19). He personally witnessed Satan's expulsion (being exiled) from heaven and we need to "see" Satan falling, as well. He has been stripped of his authority, and the authority that Adam had lost was being given back to mankind. As we are united with God, He is using us to deal with Satan's rebellion today, just as was purposed from the very beginning of time.

Jesus was saying to the seventy that we are to trample the enemy and keep him on his belly, eating dust! *Trample* means "to have physical and mental ability." The Holy Spirit has empowered us with physical and mental ability to deal with the enemy. A promise was given to David that the enemy would not be able to outwit him (see Psalm 89:22). We can be confident of that very thing, as well. The enemy cannot outwit us. We win!

It is important to note that when Jesus defeated Satan, He did not annihilate him. From humanity's inception, God declared that part of taking dominion over the earth would be to subdue (war against and tread underfoot) any hostile force that would raise itself up against the plans and purposes of God. This is still the believer's calling. Why did He permit Satan, whose head is already crushed, to remain on earth? God has left him here for us to demonstrate and enforce the victory of Christ. Jesus said: "To him who overcomes I will grant to sit with Me on My throne, as I also overcame and sat down with My Father on His throne. 'He who has an ear, let him hear what the Spirit says to the churches'" (Revelation 3:21, 22). He set the pattern. As He overcame, we can also overcome! We are here to fulfill His eternal plan until He deals

> *The enemy cannot outwit us.*
> *We win!*
> PSAlm 89:22

with Satan in the final days. Until that time we truly are "the enforcers."

Satan is a defeated foe, but God is raising up a Church, a Bride "meet" (suitable) for her Bridegroom. This "raising up" entails a learning to war, an entering into battle to "possess the Kingdom" we have already been given, a growing to maturity as we walk in His authority. Satan has been left on earth that, through the conflict, the Church might be *strengthened,* not defeated; and he will remain only as long as he serves God's purposes.

A Great Awakening

Women are Satan's enemy in a very profound and real way. For this reason, God has been awakening women to the crucial role we play in His overall plan in the earth to see the Church come into the fullness of His purpose. It is also why the enemy tries to keep women in what he thinks of as "their place," to silence us, to make us unsure of who we are and why we are here. He does not want us to discover and fulfill our true purpose. He fears the female gender and understands that our strength will be his undoing. An even greater fear is that the Church will discover the combined strength of the genders merging their anointings together as God purposed from the beginning, thereby moving in a united way to expose and conquer his evil doings and enforcing the ultimate victory Christ died to give us. *All* power has been given unto us!

We are living in a day of increased revelation. It is a time when God is bringing us into significant alignment with heaven. He will have a Body that truly displays His light and glory in the earth, as spoken of in Isaiah 60. He is redeeming and restoring all things unto Himself.

Today is a new day and we are seeing His work of restoration all around us. He is restoring His Body. God is lifting up the heads and arms of women around the world in extraordinary ways. He has been gathering a powerful prayer force in the earth that has been awakened to its divine purpose. He is causing us to be raised up in strength, health, vitality, and wholeness! He is bringing us into a greater understanding of why He created us and who He has called us be. He is awakening us to the great sense of destiny that is ours and leading us into the fulfillment of the purposes for which He created us—dealing with the ancient curse.

Women, in a very real way, are at the sharp end of the fight with the enemy.... It is time for women to understand and walk in the strength of that call.

Women, in a very real way, are at the sharp end of the fight with the enemy. The ancient curse was spoken to Satan regarding the woman following her exposure of him. It is time for women to understand and walk in the strength of that call. The greatest victory will be when men "see" the strength and purpose of our place and we begin to walk together as purposed from the beginning.

Acts 3:21 says that the heavens will actually hold Jesus back until all things have been restored. That does not mean that all the ills of mankind will be restored. What He will restore will be His ancient purposes. The initial structure He chose and set in place. From the beginning, He told us what dominion would look like. It wasn't male dominated; it wasn't female dominated. It was the two genders, male and female, walking together in the power and strength of God's original design and purpose.

Heaven to Earth

God wants us to live heaven to earth, not earth to heaven. He wants to change your address so that you live life from a different place, a different perspective. He can reveal Himself in a glorious way in the midst of any circumstances. Graham Cooke puts it this way in his book, *Qualities of a Spiritual Warrior:* "Spiritual warriors know that every situation has been designed for us to discover God's Presence and find appropriate access, using our circumstances. . . . Warriors are responsive towards God, not reactive to their circumstances. . . . Warriors see everything as an opportunity to grow, to learn, and to increase faith."[4] I have also heard Graham say that warriors "have taken their own internal territory." What an exciting way to live! We get to choose how we will live! Will we live by our circumstances or by the Word of God?

When a difficult situation recently occurred in my own life, I so clearly sensed Him saying to me, "Let not your heart be troubled. Believe!" There was such an incredible sense of peace in the midst of the storm. I didn't work at it or try to rev it up. It came out of a living relationship with an all-sufficient God. Remember what Jesus said to Thomas: "Don't be unbelieving. Believe." Peace is a strong weapon of warfare. Peace indicates where the focus of our hearts and minds is and where our trust is. That is why Isaiah stated: "The steadfast of mind Thou wilt keep in perfect peace, because he trusts in Thee" (Isaiah 26:3, NASB). God wants us to have both inward peace and outward peace—peace in the midst of any event or circumstance because He is utterly trustworthy. This truly is living from the Tree of Life, the life of Jesus. This is overcoming life.

I want to encourage you to look at your life from a

heavenly perspective. The difficulties you are encountering are intended for a divine purpose: God is increasing your authority. He is strengthening you, sharpening you, preparing you for greater purpose than you have ever known.

God is stretching many of us right now. We feel pressure on every side, and the reason for this is that God wants us to rise in the authority He has given us. He is bringing forth pure gold in our lives out of the pressures we now face. He is strengthening us on the inside so we can know Him better and represent Him more accurately in the world, in the midst of the difficult days in which we live.

I cannot encourage you strongly enough to press through the barriers and opposition currently before you. Whether it's more bills than money at the end of the month, a crisis of health or well-being, or a life that has become dull and difficult, you must press through. We must press through for each other. Let me explain. The Body of Christ is made up of individual people, yet as His Body we are a corporate entity. The Body of Christ is only as strong as each individual member. He is bringing us corporately into a greater place of victory and authority. All of us must rule over our enemies individually so we can experience victory corporately, as God's people.

> *Overcomers are not a "special class" of people; they are those who conform to the original plan of God.*

Revelation 12 speaks about the posture of the Church in this way: "They overcame him by the blood of the Lamb and by the word of their testimony, and they did not love their lives to the death" (v. 11). He has given us the power to overcome. Overcomers are not a "special class" of people; they are those who conform to the original plan of God.

Summary

- Jesus did not strip Satan of his power at the cross; He dealt with his authority.
- When Jesus died, the enemy appeared to have gained the right to rule on earth. When Jesus rose from the dead with the keys of death and hell, He returned to humanity our God-given right to rule over the enemy on earth.
- Satan is defeated, but God allows him to continue to operate on earth because He is raising up a Church, a Bride suitable for her Bridegroom.
- God is awakening the Church to many things in this hour and leading us into the fulfillment of the purposes for which He created us: dealing with the ancient curse.
- View your life and your circumstances from a heavenly perspective.

Questions

1. In your own words, what is the difference between power and authority?
2. Why does God allow Satan to continue to operate on earth? What are you learning and growing in as you journey through life in a fallen world?
3. What specific circumstance in your life do you need to view from a heavenly perspective? Take some time now to think about how God sees this situation.

7

Prophetic Purposes

Prophecy is history written in advance, as Graham Cooke says and I have mentioned; it declares the intentionality of God.

You and I are living in a day in which His prophetic purposes are unfolding in ways we have not seen before. He has spoken His intention from the beginning of time. We have the privileged position of not only being able to witness this work, but to participate in it.

Today, centuries and generations removed from Eve—the first enemy of Satan—a whole host of women are arising as his foes. These are women whose hearts are turned toward God, who understand their value and significance as women, who walk in their God-given authority, who embrace their place in God's eternal plan, who have begun to see things from His perspective, and who understand what it means to contend for His purposes to come to pass in their individual lives and in the nations of the world.

Ephesians 1:11 tells us that He "works all things according to the counsel of His will." That's not just a few things, not even most things, but *all things*. God does *everything* with the fulfillment of His plan in mind. He overlooks nothing. He does not waste time or motion. Every detail fits together for the ultimate purpose and plan of God to be fulfilled. We may not understand the events that are taking place in our lives or in the world around us, but one thing we can know is that God, as Master Builder, is always at work bringing about His master plan.

No Purpose Withheld

No story in the Bible more clearly makes the point that God is a God of purpose than the Old Testament account of Job. Through a time of tremendous testing, Job came into a revelation that increased his understanding of God. He stated that he had "heard of [God] by the hearing of the ear" (Job 42:5). He understood that God was a God who could do anything (see Job 42:2), then went on to say, "But now my eye sees You" (Job 42:5).

What was it that Job saw but did not understand as he walked through his incredible time of trial? Can you imagine the temptation to doubt God's love as he lost everything—property, health, and his children? How the enemy loves to ride on the back of such destruction in our lives. How he loves to whisper his lies into our minds, causing us to wonder if God even knows our names. How he endeavors to speak against the eternal goodness of God. His goal continues in the same pattern it had in the beginning—to cause doubt and ultimately separation from God by introducing lies about God's character and His nature.

But in the midst of Job's trial, he had a revelation of truth about God that brought clarity to his already amazing stance of faith and trust in the Almighty. He came to see that *God is only a God of purpose* (see Job 42:2). What He purposes to do, He always accomplishes.[1] There is no purpose of His that can be withheld from Him. He has a purpose for His creation. He has a purpose and destiny for your life personally. It may feel at times that you have been forgotten, overlooked, not cared about. You cannot see how your destiny and all the prophetic words spoken over your life could ever come to pass. You feel as though you are looking at a mountain that is unmovable. Remember, situations are not just there to be resolved. They are allowed to bring us into a revelation of God and an experience of Him at that point!

What He purposes to do, He always accomplishes. There is no purpose of His that can be withheld from Him.

Job found out that his destiny could not be withheld, first of all from God, and secondly, from himself. Your destiny cannot be withheld from you, because it cannot be withheld from Him. You have a destiny. He has spoken it over your life. He is working in your life to bring it to pass.

It's about God

Even as David realized that God was leading him in paths of righteousness for *His name's sake* (see Psalm 23:3), he was declaring the same truth that Job discovered. This is more about God than it is about us! He leads us in "right paths" or paths of righteousness, for His name's sake. He is leading, guiding, and constantly moving on His own behalf in our lives. You can count on it. It is His nature. It is His plan. This realization will change your prayer life. It will cause your heart to be lifted up in celebration and worship as you journey through life. You will find yourself praying heaven-to-earth prayers. You will hear yourself declaring God's truth over your life and the situations you face. This realization will cause the Church to rise up in the victorious stance He purposed for us from the beginning of time. It is all about *Him!*

This is more about God than it is about us!

God's destined purpose for the Body of Christ will come to pass, not because we are mighty in ourselves, but because it was the plan He conceived as His eternal plan before the foundation of the world. It is more about Him than it is about us. We simply get to be the ones who participate with Him in this grand unfolding of His plan in this hour.

The Bigger Picture

When we refer to "the Fall," we often view it as the starting point of God's purpose on earth. In doing this, we then interpret human history from the point of the Fall. This thinking leads us to perceive that God's primary purpose on earth was the redemption of mankind, that there was no other goal. We become very "man centered" instead of "God centered." It becomes "all about me." He came to save me, bless me, and take care of me. Of course, these things are, in fact, the heart of the Gospel. However, if our perspective never becomes larger than ourselves, we will live with a short-sighted view, a "self"-centered view of God's purposes.

Redemption is never to be minimized. But we need to move beyond ourselves and our needs to see the bigger picture. God had a plan from the beginning of time. The enemy moved to disrupt that plan and bring chaos. Redemption was incorporated into God's plan to bring us back to His original purpose. We need to move from a self-centered focus to a God-centered focus that reaches from eternity past, to eternity present, into eternity future.

God's intention has always been to have a Body—a group of people in the earth who would love Him and follow Him—so that through them He might make Himself known in the earth and bring the authority of heaven to earth. His purpose extended beyond the first man and woman in the garden and reached out to every human being who will align with His glorious plan. We are those people. His glorious purpose is unfolding. It is an awesome time to be alive!

A Prophetic Purpose Fulfilled

God's eternal plan, spoken at the beginning of time, seemed so disrupted. How would that purpose be fulfilled? Understanding that He is only a God of purpose, we know that He would have taken "all things" into account, and nothing of His plan would be lost. He had spoken it first to a man and a woman. Would the recovery come through a man and a woman? Abraham was the man chosen of God as the starting point in His plan of redemption and His work of recovery. Romans 4:17 tells us that Abraham is the father of all those who believe. Through Abraham, God would turn the tide for all mankind. Redemption was accomplished by the death and resurrection of Jesus, but its starting point was with Abraham.

We hear the prophetic purpose of God being spoken forth in the earth. Genesis 12 gives us a clear indication of how far reaching this calling was. He would become the father of many nations. In him all the families of the earth would be blessed. See the pattern set forth in the garden being repeated now to Abraham: Live in the land; express God there; and carry out the authority of heaven in that land. Sounds like the plan spoken to the first man and woman.

God has always wanted a people for Himself. It started with Adam and Eve, and then, with the calling of Abraham, a mighty prophetic purpose of God hung in the atmosphere waiting to be fulfilled. God's redemptive plan would come through this man. However, there was a problem. His wife Sarah was barren! Romans 4:19 states that his own body was dead as well, because he was a hundred years old. Even if Abraham's body was restored to life, there remained a problem—barrenness and deadness in his wife's womb, no ability to receive the prophetic seed of life that would bring to pass Abraham's destiny and the prophetic purpose of God. God's recovery plan for mankind could not come to pass until the barrenness in Sarah was reversed.

God has always wanted a people for Himself.

Think about the fact that Scripture includes two significant instances when God prophetically spoke His purposes pointing toward the First Coming of Jesus. In each case, He chose a man *and* a woman: Abraham and Sarah, who would bring forth Isaac, the promised heir of the covenant (see

Genesis 17:16–21) and a type of Christ. Zacharias and Elizabeth, would bring forth John the Baptist, the one of whom it is said: he will "make ready a people prepared for the Lord" (Luke 1:17). His purpose was to herald the arrival of the Messiah. In each of these cases, the women were barren. In order for God's plan to move forward, pointing toward the First Coming of His Son, Jesus, He first had to deal with the barrenness in these women. Unless God moved in their lives in this way, His prophetic word, His promise, His ultimate intention, would not come to pass. God's plan for the world was—and remains—intimately connected to the lives of men and women, and the destinies of men and women are often intertwined for the fulfillment of His purposes.

God is quickening and reversing the spiritual barrenness in women in this hour as we have never seen before.

The same is true today. Prophetic words will remain only empty words until heaven intervenes and quickens those words to life. Destinies will go unfulfilled and God's plan will go unfulfilled—for both men and women—until heaven reaches down and breathes life on those words that will cause us to walk together in unity and power, as He planned from the beginning.

Again, God underscores the power of the man and woman, together, in bringing about His eternal plan. He intends no less for men and women today. I believe God is quickening and reversing the spiritual barrenness in women in this hour as we have never seen before. This is for the ultimate purpose of restoring the corporate Body, male and female, to life and fruitfulness, so that together we can participate with heaven in this final stage of His unfolding plan. Let me share, from a "front row seat," what I see happening in the lives of women today.

It's Happening Everywhere

James 4:7 speaks of God's order of dealing with Satan. "Submit to God. Resist the devil and he will flee from you." From the beginning, this was the order of things. Partake of His life, then resist the enemy and he will flee, run away from us. This is how we become a mighty force for God upon the earth.

When I write of "a mighty force for God upon the earth," I do not mean legions of angels. I mean real flesh-and-blood women and men who so understand their significance and their authority that they have given their hearts and lives to the fulfillment of God's purposes. I've seen them; I know them; they are everywhere.

I believe we are living in a day when we are seeing a corporate calling forth and a worldwide awakening in the lives of women (yes, and men) in a unique and unprecedented way. It is unprecedented because never, in all of history, has a move quite like this occurred among women globally. As we look back in history, we can see that God has always used women. However, it has been primarily on a singular basis. There have been the Hannah's, Deborah's, and Esther's who have been wonderfully used of God in furthering His plan in the earth, sometimes without even realizing it. But never has there been this kind of a worldwide awakening. Because He works all things after the counsel of His will, this indicates to me that He is up to something! It is something glorious.

The backbone of many societies in the world today—and throughout history—has been women. We are the ones who raise the children; we instill into them their traditions, their ways of thinking, and their belief systems. In these ways, women perpetuate values, ideals, and mindsets. This is true in Christianity, Judaism, Islam, and many other religious and cultural expressions. When God captures the hearts of women, He also gains access to the hearts and minds of men and children—and that has the potential to change the world.

Summary

- God is a God of purpose. He allows difficult situations in our lives to teach us something about Himself.
- God is constantly moving in our lives for His sake, for the accomplishment of His purposes.
- We need to value all that God has done for us, while moving beyond ourselves to see what He is doing in the earth.
- God's plan for the world has always been intimately connected to the lives of men and women, and the destinies of men and women are often intertwined for the fulfillment of His purposes.
- God is healing, awakening, and calling forth women around the world today in a unique and unprecedented way.

Questions

1. What hardship or difficulty in your life has God used to reveal something about Himself to you?
2. I have stated that God's purpose for putting man

on earth certainly includes redemption, but moves beyond that. How would you describe the larger scope of God's purpose for mankind?

3.   How can you be part of a mighty force for God upon the earth?

God Has Always Used Women

Take a walk back in history with me. Even though we are in the midst of a great awakening among women in the early twenty-first century, we must remember that God has always used women in significant ways as He has carried out His plans on earth. This is evident in ancient writings of the Bible, where we read the stories of women such as Jochebed, Deborah, Hannah, Esther, Abigail, Lydia, and others. These were women who cooperated with God in furthering His plan in the earth, sometimes without even realizing it.

Jochebed: Uncommon Courage

Consider the story of Jochebed, the mother of Moses and a woman of great faith. When the edict came from Pharaoh to destroy all male Hebrew babies (see Exodus 1:22), her response sprang from a vital part of her womanhood. She must preserve the life of her son! At first reading, it looks like such a natural thing for a woman to do. Yet it was this very thing God needed, at that moment in the history of His people, to move His plan another step forward. God had sent a deliverer to His people. With the birth of Moses God had set in motion the deliverance of His people, a deliverance He had been planning for nearly 400 years. Jochebed, the mother of Moses, was doing what any mother would do, yet she was moving in great faith as she placed her baby in a basket amongst the reeds of the great Nile River. It was an act that appeared very ordinary and simple, yet it was the love, faith, and courage of Jochebed that preserved Moses to bless the world and set history in motion. The plan of God for His people seemed to hinge on the response of a woman—and Jochebed, a mother, was that woman.

Hannah: Uncommon Surrender

Consider also Hannah, a woman who struggled with infertility. Barrenness, for a woman of her day, was a source of terrible shame. Out of her pain and a deep longing to have a child, she grieved and wept before the Lord. She was a woman who, like so many women, just wanted a baby! But God was in the midst of Hannah's barrenness. He was again orchestrating something from heaven for the furtherance of His plan and purpose on the earth; and He would use this woman, her grief, and her pain, and turn it into a powerful testimony of His great faithfulness. You see, barrenness was not only Hannah's physical condition; it was also the spiritual condition of God's people. The Bible says in 1 Samuel 3:1 that *"the word of the Lord was rare in those days"* (emphasis mine). Israel as a nation was spiritually barren.

God needed a man who would have an ear to hear His voice, a heart to follow His ways—a man through whom He could speak forth His prophetic word in that hour. So God looked for someone who would participate with Him in bringing the will of heaven to earth. He found a woman! A woman who would begin to cry out and plead with Him for a child. God placed on Hannah's heart a burden that corresponded to the very burden of His own heart. There came a point when Hannah stepped out of her own need and into the purposes of God: "If You will indeed look on the affliction of Your maidservant and . . . give Your maidservant a male child, then I will give

> *God was in the midst of Hannah's barrenness.*

him to the LORD all the days of his life" (1 Samuel 1:11). That was the moment God was waiting for; those were the words He wanted to hear. He had a willing vessel. Hannah would be used of God to bring forth one of the greatest prophets Israel would ever know.

God moved on Hannah's behalf and gave her a son, Samuel. However, He was actually also moving on His own behalf to fulfill His purpose in the earth. Once again, it would seem the ongoing plan of God hinged on the response of a woman.

Esther: Uncommon Calling

Esther, a Jewess, who would one day become the queen of King Ahasuerus of Persia, is another such woman, used of God at a crucial time in history. A number of Jewish people were still living in Babylon under Persian rule at that time.

Haman, second in command to the king, had devised a plot to destroy the Jews, convincing the king to call for their execution.

Mordecai, who had brought up his uncle's daughter, Esther—who was orphaned following the deaths of her mother and father—urged her not to reveal her racial origin. Upon learning of the fate of the Jewish people, Mordecai convinced her not to remain silent on behalf of her people. Haman's plot had to be revealed. Mordecai's strong words of destiny were spoken over this beautiful young woman: "Who knows whether you have come to the kingdom for such a time as this?" (Esther 4:14).

Esther skillfully, courageously, and shrewdly moved to expose the enemy's evil plot by entering the inner court of the king's palace without proper invitation. As she stood before the king's throne, God gave her favor and, in that moment, the king extended his scepter to her. As she moved forward to touch the top of the golden scepter, the king's question moved far beyond a mere inquiry as to her appearance. "What is your request? It shall be given to you—up to half the kingdom!" (Esther 5:2, 3). The favor being extended to Esther was beyond anything she would have thought to ask for herself. The king was offering his scepter, which was the rod of a ruler, symbolizing his power.

> *Esther skillfully, courageously, and shrewdly moved to expose the enemy's evil plot.*

As the counter plot of Esther unfolded, King Ahasuerus ultimately gave Queen Esther the house of Haman, the enemy of the Jews, and the scheme he had devised against the Jews was destroyed, along with Haman himself (see Esther 8).

A decree reversing the edict of Haman over the Jewish people was released through Queen Esther, with the permission of the king, in his name, and sealed with his signet ring. She was coming in the authority of the king. What a picture of co-rulership, of extended authority, of a wise and skillful woman who was used of God to save the lives of many during a critical time. Today, the Jewish people continue to celebrate the Feast of Purim each year prior to Passover, celebrating Esther's role in the deliverance of God's people.

According to the *New Spirit-Filled Life Bible* Introduction to the Book of Esther, the lives of Esther and Mordecai are "a classic example of successful teamwork" between a man and a woman. "Their relationship portrays the unity that the Lord prayed for His disciples to experience (see John 17). The success of their individual roles, even their very survival, depended entirely upon their unity."[1] The heart and plan of God was able to be realized through these two courageous people.

Abigail: Uncommon Understanding

Abigail was the wife of a rich, but foolish, harsh, and angry man who was evil in his business dealings. She is another example of a wise and courageous woman. The Scripture describes her as a woman of good understanding and beautiful in appearance. To be spoken of as being a woman of understanding would imply that she had an understanding of God's will and His ways.

A critical situation arose between her husband Nabal and David, who was in the wilderness of Paran at that time. David, aware that it was sheep-shearing time at Nabal's, sent ten young men to make a request of Nabal in a spirit of peace. It was a feast day and David was asking Nabal to give them whatever provisions he could extend to David and his men. Nabal not only denied the request, but he also spoke scornfully of David as an insignificant man. This was David, the king of the land! David's response was immediate and his resolution bloody. He said to his men, "Every man gird on his sword. . . . Surely in vain I have protected all that this fellow has. . . . He has repaid me evil for good. May God do so, and more also, to the enemies of David, if I leave one male of all who belong to [Nabal]" (1 Samuel 25:13, 21, 22). When Abigail heard of her husband's response, she made haste, taking provision worthy of a king with her. When Abigail saw David she dismounted quickly from the donkey, fell on her face before David, and bowed down to the ground. "On me, my lord, on me let this iniquity be! And please let your maidservant speak in your ears, and hear the words of your maidservant. Please, let not my lord regard this scoundrel Nabal. For as his name is, so is he: Nabal is his name, and folly is with him!" (1 Samuel 25:24, 25). This is not an angry, vindictive woman, but a woman whose heart had been broken, touched, and turned to God. She is a woman of understanding from God's point of view.

David received her as she began to speak into his life and future destiny: "As your soul lives, . . . the LORD has held you back from coming to bloodshed and from avenging yourself with your own hand. . . . The LORD will certainly make for my lord an enduring house, because my lord fights the battles of the LORD, and

> *This is not an angry, vindictive woman, but a woman whose heart had been broken, touched, and turned to God.*

evil is not found in you throughout your days" (1 Samuel 25:26, 28).

"Then David said to Abigail: 'Blessed is the LORD God of Israel, who sent you this day to meet me! And blessed is your advice and blessed are you, because you have kept me this day from coming to bloodshed and from avenging myself with my own hand. . . . I have heeded your voice and respected your person'" (1 Samuel 25:32, 33, 35)! Abigail knew God and His ways; therefore God could use her to express His ways to others—even to the king.

Lydia: Uncommon Purpose

Lydia, a single woman and a prominent business woman in the prosperous city of Thyatira, is a striking New Testament figure who holds a significant place in the furthering of the gospel into Europe. Lydia was the first European convert of Paul's and the forerunner of a mighty host who would become followers of Christ. Her conversion was made by public confession, and immediately she and her entire household were baptized as disciples of the Lord.

Isn't it interesting that upon Paul's heeding of the Macedonian call and his arrival in Europe, he found his way to a prayer meeting and sat down and spoke to the women who met there (see Acts 16:13)? Although Lydia was, at that time, sincerely religious, she was not yet a Christian. This meeting of Paul and Lydia was surely a "God encounter" and the beginning of God's plan to bring the gospel to the continent of Europe. Again, a woman was used of God in a most significant way for the furtherance of His eternal plan.

God Is Up to Something

Though we can clearly see in Scripture and we know from history that God has always chosen women to help bring forth His purposes on earth—either alone or in partnership with men—let me reiterate that I do not believe there has ever been the kind of awakening among women that we have seen in the last 30 to 40 years.

One of the names of God is Jehovah Jireh, the God who sees ahead and provides: He sees the need, He prepares for the need, so that when the hour comes, He has already made provision for what is needed in that season. God has been preparing women, as evidenced by this awakening, for their role in bringing forth what is on His heart for the Church and for the world, in the coming days.

This unprecedented move of God's Spirit in the lives of women has to do with the ultimate plan of God being fulfilled in the earth—because He purposes to join men and women in wholeness, in health, without fear, without intimidation, walking side by side. I believe this move of God ultimately has to do with the destiny of the Church being fulfilled. Jehovah Jireh has made provision for what is needed in this hour!

> *...He purposes to join men and women in wholeness, in health, without fear, without intimidation, walking side by side.*

The Essence of God's Purpose

Like Sarah and Elizabeth who needed God's quickening touch, another woman also illustrates the essence of God's purpose for women down through the ages. Her story in Luke 13:10–17 tells us that the bent over woman, "could in no way raise herself up." She had suffered with a spirit of infirmity for eighteen long years. The word *infirmity* means "unable to function as purposed and designed."

It is interesting to note where Jesus found this woman. It was in the synagogue. As He was teaching there one day, His attention was drawn to her in the midst of the crowd. As He moved toward her, He began to speak words of life over her. And as He did, her heart was lifted up. Her head was lifted up. Her arms were lifted up, and she began to glorify God! The men standing nearby questioned Jesus because He had healed on the Sabbath. His response to them was, "Ought not this woman, being a daughter of Abraham, whom Satan has bound—think of it—for eighteen years, be loosed from this bond on the Sabbath?" (v. 16). I believe the Lord is speaking these words to women in the Church today. In essence, He is saying: "Ought not these handmaidens, these women who have been bent over and bound, be set free?" In this unprecedented move, Jesus is speaking words of freedom over women's lives. In response, our hearts and hands are lifted, and we are bringing glory to God in the earth.

> *She was healed and set free because Jesus took the initiative to make her whole.*

The enemy, knowing the significant place God has given women, has feared our rising to our purpose and, therefore, has sought to keep us blinded, bound, and crippled. Luke 13:11 tells us that the bent over woman *could do nothing to raise herself up.* Unless God moved on her behalf, she would forever stay in that bent-over, crippled, limited position and would be unable to function as purposed and designed. She was healed and set free because Jesus took the initiative to make her whole.

I believe the Spirit of God has once again taken the initiative toward women in this hour, because, indeed, He is doing a unique thing in the earth. He is quickening women to life in a way we have not witnessed before. He is awakening; He is stirring; He is renewing; He is equipping; and He is positioning women in such a way that we will step in alongside our brothers to fulfill His great Kingdom purposes.

We have read of God's using men and women together in days of old—Abraham and Sarah, and Zacharias and Elizabeth—and of His bringing life through them in ways that pointed toward and eventually culminated in the First Coming of Jesus Christ to earth.

In this hour, as events all around us point toward the Second Coming of Jesus, God is again touching the barrenness in women's lives. In areas where we have not been fruitful—because our influence has been ignored, our voices silenced, or our presence unwelcome—God is giving us the power to bring life. He is restoring our maleness and our femaleness back to what He purposed it to be so we can function in wholeness with one another. As He does so, greater restoration will come to the Church so His ultimate intention can be fulfilled in and through us.

Summary

- God has always used women to accomplish His purposes.
- Jochebed, Esther, Hannah, Abigail, and Lydia all played specific, important roles in the fulfillment of God's plan for His people and the world.
- God knows what the world needs in this hour and has made provision for it. Part of His provision in-

volves the unprecedented awakening taking place among women today.

- Just as Jesus moved toward the infirm woman in order to heal her, the Spirit of God is once again taking the initiative to heal, restore, and empower women so we can be used to fulfill His purposes.

Questions

1. Think of Jochebed. In what ways are you a person of uncommon courage?
2. Think of Hannah. In what ways are you a person of uncommon surrender?
3. Think of Esther. In what ways are you a person of uncommon calling?
4. Think of Abigail. In what ways are you a person of uncommon understanding?
5. Think of Lydia. In what ways are you a person of uncommon purpose?

Working Together to Accomplish God's Purposes

The story of Deborah and Barak presents an excellent picture of male and female working together for victory, restoration, and the accomplishment of God's purposes for His people. Let me remind you of a time when Israel was doing evil in the sight of the Lord, and once again the Lord gave the people into the hand of their enemies. This time it was King Jabin of Canaan who for 20 years "harshly oppressed the children of Israel" (Judges 4:3), until in their desperation they cried out to the Lord for help. And God sent help—by way of a woman. Her name was Deborah.

Deborah and Barak

Deborah was a prophetess, which speaks of her relationship with God and ability to hear His voice. She was also noted as the wife of Lapidoth, which indicates she had a proper relationship with her husband. She was also a judge, or leader, in Israel. Only two people are mentioned in Scripture as being both judge and prophet. Samuel was one, Deborah the other.

Though Deborah had a prominent position in society and also had the call of God on her life, she seems to have been comfortable in her role as wife and homemaker. Scripture does not indicate that she chafed under this role, even though she was obviously a very gifted stateswoman. Whether Deborah had children is not mentioned. If she did, they may have reached a certain maturity by this time in her life.

I believe Deborah had the love and encouragement of her husband. In her day and age, it is unlikely she could have become the leader she did without his support. Apparently, he was secure enough and humble enough to recognize God's call on her life and allow her to be used in an incredible, powerful way. Such freedom did not diminish his identity at all—she was, after all, referred to as "Lapodith's wife." Because he is mentioned by name, he, too, was likely a man of some renown.

Deborah was the political and judicial head of the nation and was greatly respected by those who served her, as well as by all Israel. Her exemplary leadership abilities did not spring solely from natural talent; rather, I believe they were the result of her close relationship with God.

As a prophetess, she was able to hear the word and the heart of the Lord and then declare it to others. Her name literally means "bee." Research indicates that the Hebrew root of her name, *debar*, connotes a sense of being able to put things in order and having instincts for orderly systems that will work. No doubt those abilities were greatly needed during her day in Israel!

Her exemplary leadership abilities did not spring solely from natural talent; rather, I believe they were the result of her close relationship with God.

From all we have learned about a woman's design, the way God made women to function, we should not be surprised that Deborah's leadership was specifically linked, even by her name, to her ability to "speak"—to hear and to communicate the word of the Lord with clarity and understanding.

Because of her intimate relationship with God, she was also a warrior, a military leader who moved with great wisdom and authority. Once Deborah was assured she had heard from God, she moved quickly to put His mandate into action.

In her story, we read that she had heard by the Spirit of God that the time had come to end the oppressive rule of King Jabin. She summoned Barak, commander of the armies of Israel, a man who is listed among the great men of faith in Hebrews 11. Deborah asks, "Has not the LORD God of Israel commanded, 'Go and deploy troops . . . and I will deliver [the commander of Jabin's army] into your hand'?" (Judges 4:6, 7).

Barak's response has always intrigued me. Though he is a military man, a man of great strength and experienced in military conflicts, this time something is different about him. His reply bears witness to his great admiration and confidence in Deborah: "If you will go with me, then I will go; but if you will not go with me, I will not go!" (v. 8).

Even though Barak is told he will not receive full honor for the victory (in this particular battle a woman named Jael will deliver the death blow to the enemy's head [see vv. 9, 21]), he is not moved. The issue for Barak and for the armies of Israel was not whether a woman was present on the battlefield, but the successful outcome of the war. Clearly, he cared more for the welfare of the nation than for his personal reputation. He realized that the greater good of the Nation of Israel was at stake. He also knew that their combined efforts (his and Deborah's), each bringing their particular strengths, would ensure the victory. And victors they were.

"So on that day [the day Barak and Deborah joined forces and went to war against their enemies] God subdued Jabin king of Canaan in the presence of the children of Israel. And the hand of the children of Israel grew stronger and stronger against Jabin king of Canaan, until they had destroyed Jabin king of Canaan" (vv. 23, 24).

What a celebration followed! "Then Deborah and Barak . . . sang on that day, saying: 'When leaders lead in Israel, when the people willingly offer themselves, bless the LORD!'" (5:1, 2).

The leaders had led, and the Lord was blessed. The issue was not male or female; the issue was the anointing, the call and equipping of God that made them leaders, male *and* female.

Unity and Restoration

Just as God used men and women together to bear fruit to accomplish His purposes in Deborah and Barak's day, so He is calling men and women to work together again, to bring forth His purposes in our day. As we consider the importance of gender reconciliation and the work of restoration that God is doing in our midst today, we must remember that the bottom line of everything Jesus came to do was to restore relationship—with God and with each other. He came to "destroy the works of the devil" (1 John 3:8). The works of the devil, then and now, include alienated, fragmented relationships. Sin, at its core, is the failure to love others. All the problems of the world—from wars between nations, the fracturing of our culture, divisions in the Church, or divorce between couples—are problems of relationship.

When our relationships are right, when we are walking in true intimacy with God and others, we will have a testimony before the world that those who are truly seeking the meaning of life will be unable to resist. It is this, our genuine love for one another, that Jesus said would testify of His life in

> *... we must remember that the bottom line of everything Jesus came to do was to restore relationship—with God and with each other.*

us (see John 13:34, 35). His disciples would not be recognized by physical healings, not by miracles, signs, or wonders, as wonderful and exciting as these are, but by love.

In the atmosphere of such love, God's anointing for the miraculous and the power that "breaks the yoke" of our enemies is poured out. Psalm 133 declares: "Behold, how good and how pleasant it is for brethren to dwell together in unity! It is like the precious oil upon the head, running down on the beard, the beard of Aaron, running down on the edge of his garments. It is like the dew of Hermon, descending upon the mountains of Zion; for there the LORD commanded the blessing—life forevermore" (vv. 1–3).

The oil mentioned in Psalm 133 represents the anointing of the Holy Spirit. In unity there is anointing and life. In unity God commands the blessing! Until that unity comes to the very core of God's creation—male and female—it will not have reached its complete fulfillment. It is no accident of nature that it takes both male and female to bring forth life. This was God's design. The absence of either produces emptiness, barrenness, and impotence. The world will not fully see Jesus until the foundation of His house—the God-intended partnership between male and female—is fully repaired.

> *The world will not fully see Jesus until the foundation of His house—the God-intended partnership between male and female—is fully repaired.*

What will be our response as a Church in this day and hour, at this most turbulent time in our history, when God is calling us to increased presence and spiritual effectiveness in this dark and dying world? Let us consider the question and then respond to each other, male and female, as Barak did to Deborah: "I will not go without you!" Indeed, God would say, "You *cannot* go without each other. The life, the power, the victory will come from your union! It is there I gave My blessing. From the beginning I have said, 'Let them, male and female, rule and have dominion over the earth.' I have not changed My plan. As I have said, so shall it be!"

Summary

- Deborah and Barak are an excellent example of a man and a woman working together effectively to fulfill God's purposes.

- God's people needed a victory, and Barak knew it was not possible without the combination of his and Deborah's strengths together.

- God still uses men and women, such as Deborah and Barak, to partner with each other to accomplish His purposes today. This is why the restoration of relationship between the genders is so important.

- God blesses unity.

Questions

1. What historic or modern-day examples of teamwork between men and women can you think of?

2. What unique strengths did Deborah and Barak each bring to the crisis their nation faced? In other words, how did each contribute to the victory God's people needed?

3. What relationships in your life need to be made right? In what ways do you need to come into unity with someone else?

10

The Restoration

When Eve offered Adam the fruit of the tree of the knowledge of good and evil, and when he partook of it, sin entered the human race. Where sin is, broken relationships are sure to follow. The sin in the garden opened wide a door of distrust between the genders, creating a gap in relationship that still needs to be closed in many arenas, as God restores both men and women to the fullness of His purpose in creating us—male and female.

Today millions of women are in bondage because of Eve's deception and subsequent involvement in sin in the garden. But that act of hers has been redeemed. Nevertheless, because sin has run rampant through nations, cultures, mindsets, and the systems of societies, millions of women remain captive to sin and brokenness, as I shared earlier.

We must remember, however, that no purpose of God's can be withheld from Him (see Job 42:2). What He has purposed will come to pass, and He has purposed that the genders—male and female—be reconciled to reflect His full image in the earth together. Indeed, God is moving mightily in the lives of women today. He is saying, "I will have a body of women in the earth who have given their hearts to Me in a full-fledged way. They are redeemed; they are restored; they are awakened; they are aware. They understand My plan. They understand why I have called them." God is raising up women who understand that He is looking for any individual woman or company of women who will cooperate with Him in bringing forth the plan He spoke of in Genesis 1, 2, and 3. This matter of reconciling male and female is the part of the nature of the war we see around us on earth and the war we sense around us in the spiritual realm. It is the purpose of the restoration that is underway as God heals, strengthens, and equips women to serve His purposes and advance His Kingdom alongside our brothers.

> *He has purposed that the genders—male and female—be reconciled to reflect His full image in the earth together.*

Restoration in Perspective

The restoration God desires for women is not about positions on church boards: it is not about whether we can be pastors or leaders and still be "doctrinally correct." We can (and do) see women in all these positions in churches around the world. Today, as in the early New Testament

Church, we have women such as Junia, who was named among the apostles in Romans 16:7. We have women such as Phoebe, a deacon (or deaconess), specifically identified as a leader or manager of the things of God who, at times, worked with Paul (see Romans 16:1, 2). There are women such as Priscilla, a teacher of both men and women (see Acts 18:24–26).

Yet we are still missing God's heart. Although we have women functioning in all these roles, we are still nervous about it, uncomfortable, unsure that it is fully appropriate. The reason is that the issue goes much deeper than that. It is not about whether women can teach or hold offices in the Church. It is about the image of God, the likeness and glory of God being manifested in the Church, male and female. It is about both coming together as He designed from the beginning. It is about respect that comes from a heart revelation of the vital contribution of both male and female, and the devastation that results when either is missing or not functioning. Only as we walk together will we be fully equipped to expose the works of darkness and counter the lies the enemy has perpetrated throughout the ages.

Toward the Reconciled Church

As we move toward becoming the Church in which male and female are fully reconciled, we see that we have been in a time of transition. We have outgrown the past and present experience we have had, and it is time for a new day to dawn. As I travel the nations of the earth, I notice a restlessness in God's people, a holy dissatisfaction, a discomfort with the way things are in the world and in the Church. I believe the reason we are restless is that God has placed within our hearts a desire to move forward. He is taking us from our current position to the place of destiny He has purposed for us. Just as God brought the Israelites out, that He might bring them in to a good and a large place (see Deuteronomy 6:23), so we, too, as His people are leaving the place we have been and are moving toward something greater.

As the Israelites were about to cross over into their inheritance, Joshua tells us that, on the third day, the officers ran through the camp saying, "When you see the ark of the covenant of the LORD your God . . . you shall set out from your place and go after it" (Joshua 3:3). In other words, "Get ready to get going!" As the Church, we are about to cross over into what God has spoken and promised to us. But like the Israelites, we have not been this way before. Therefore, we, like the Israelites, must keep His presence before us and follow where He leads us. God called Abraham to leave his home and go to a land He would show him. Abraham obeyed, not knowing where he was going. I believe we are in a similar place today. We are certain He is guiding us, but we must keep His presence before us as He leads us to our destiny.

I believe the reason we are restless is that God has placed within our hearts a desire to move forward.

A Day with No End

Genesis 2 gives us a picture of the people God desires us to be, as it reveals what He intended for Himself had sin never entered the picture of humanity. The chapter opens with the seventh day, where we read that God finished His work and then He rested. The seventh day is the only day that has no recorded end in Scripture. All of the previous days in the creation account had a beginning and an end. But on the seventh day, God rested because He had set in place His perfect plan, and *nothing* could prevent this plan from coming to pass—not sin, not time, not flesh, nor the devil. Let Satan do his worst and God would still rest. He had set in place His perfect plan and it would be fulfilled. Hebrews 4:3 states that His works were finished from the foundations of the world!

Through Genesis 2, we see the Church walking in the seventh-day rest, not striving, but resting and confident in God's finished work. We see the Church living in a life-union with God. We see the Church walking in unity with one another, male and female. We see the Church walking in authority, subduing and taking dominion in the earth. And finally, we see the Church fulfilling the mandate God had given us through the power of the life that was to have come from the Tree of Life, which represents the life of Jesus.

This is God's plan. This is the reconciled Church!

Is what God's Word says—is what He has declared—really going to come to pass? It is being pushed to the limit and, as this spirit of anti-christ is arising and tensions increase in the earth and the Church, God is forming a Body of people who are strong, whole, and passionate for Him and for His purposes. He is causing women to arise. He is causing men and women to come together in the way He purposed from the beginning, because He is going to showcase His authority, His power, His divine nature, His divine presence in the earth. There is an alignment of genders, a merging of anointings, taking place in this hour that will bring forth a powerful victory on earth. It was intended from the beginning; it is the true face of dominion; and it may well be necessary for the Second Coming of Jesus Christ.

The place where the Church has lived is too small. We have not reflected the full image of God or begun to live as the spotless Bride for which Jesus will return. However, God is making ready a glorious Bride, and we are part of it. He is changing and expanding and purifying the Church, setting His house in order. He is bringing forth in the earth a people who will arise in His strength, His power, His authority, such as we have never seen in all of history.

O Lord, let there be a great restoration such as has never been seen in the earth before, male and female, the foundation of Your house, joined together in respect, in honor, valuing one another as indispensable to Your plan. Let us go forth in might, in power, in the full revelation of Jesus Christ on earth, according to Your original design, fulfilling our mandate declared at the beginning of time. For Your sake, Lord, for Your glory, for Your purpose, we pray! Amen and amen. So be it!

Summary

- Sin leads to broken relationships.
- God wants to restore broken relationships between men and women, both individually and corporately.
- The restoration God wants for women is not to elevate the status or position of women in the Church. It is intended to help reveal the fullness of His image to the world.
- As the Church, we have outgrown our past experience. It is time for something new.
- God's plan is for the Church to walk in confident rest and bold authority and for us to walk in unity

with Himself and with others. This is the reconciled Church.

Questions

1. How has sin led to broken relationships in your life?
2. What is God's purpose for the restoration of women?
3. In your own words, how would you describe the reconciled Church?

Notes

Chapter 2

1. Donald Grey Barnhouse, *The Invisible War* (Grand Rapids, MI: Zondervan Publishing House, 1965), 51.

2. George Ricker Berry, The Interlinear Literal Translation of the Hebrew Old Testament (Grand Rapids, MI: Kregel Publications, 1975).

3. Watchman Nee, *Messenger of the Cross* (New York: Christian Fellowship Publishers, 1980), 136-137.

Chapter 3

1. *Theological Wordbook of the Old Testament,* R. Laird Harris, Gleason L. Archer Jr., and Bruce K Waltke, eds. (Chicago: Moody Press, 1980), #1598.

Chapter 6

1. Dutch Sheets, *Authority in Prayer* (Bloomington, MN: Bethany House Publishers, 2006), 11.

2. Ibid., 11.

3. Ibid., 20.

4. Graham Cooke, *Qualities of a Spiritual Warrior* (Vacaville, CA: Brilliant Book House, 2008), 118, 179.

Chapter 7

1. My comments on Job 42:2 are inspired by Bob Sorge's book, *The Fire of Delayed Answers* (Canandiagua, NY: Oasis House, 1996), 40-41.

Chapter 8

1.   Jack W. Hayford, ed., *New Spirit-Filled Life Bible,* (Nashville, TN: Thomas Nelson Publishers), 633.